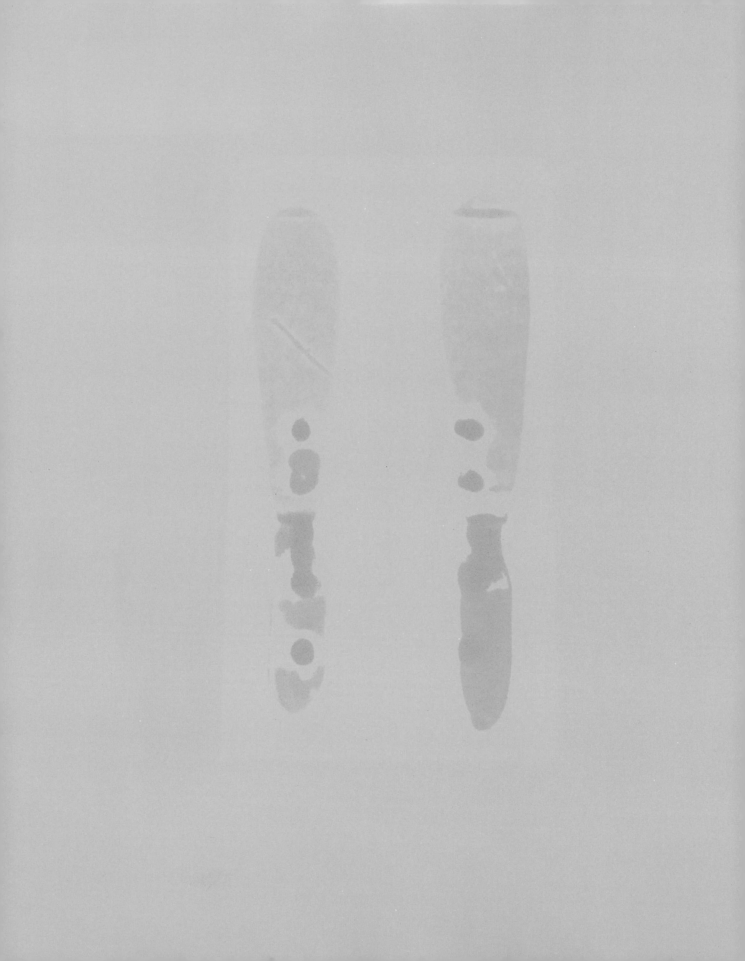

Big
Birds

Big Birds

Denise Casey

Photographs by
Jackie Gilmore

COBBLEHILL BOOKS / Dutton

New York

For Evan.   — D.C.

Acknowledgments

We would like to thank Eric Stone of Teton Science School in Kelly, Wyoming, and Gary Backhouse of the Victoria Department of Conservation and Environment in Melbourne, Australia, for their helpful comments on the text.

D. C.

Thanks to Education and Public Relations Director Mark Stackhouse of Tracy Aviary, Salt Lake City, Utah, for his considerable time and assistance in photographing birds at the aviary; Utah's Hogle Zoo, Salt Lake City, for permission to use photographs of zoo birds and to docents for assistance in handling them; to Cheyenne Mountain Zoo, Colorado Springs, Colorado, for permission to use photographs of their zoo birds; and to Peabody Museum of Natural History at Yale University for permission to photograph the Giant Moa Exhibit.

J. G.

Library of Congress Cataloging-in-Publication Data
Casey, Denise.
    Big birds/Denise Casey; photographs by Jackie Gilmore.
        p.   cm.
    Includes index.
    Summary: Introduces, in simple text and photographs,
the characteristics, habits, and natural environment of such large birds
as the brown pelican, ostrich, emperor penguin, and bald eagle.
    ISBN 0-525-65121-7
    1. Birds--Juvenile literature. [1. Birds.] I. Gilmore, Jackie, ill.
II. Title.
    QL676.2.C37 1993   598--dc20   92-17275   CIP   AC

Published in the United States by Cobblehill Books, an affiliate of Dutton Children's Books,
a division of Penguin Books USA Inc., 375 Hudson Street, New York, New York 10014
Designed by Charlotte Staub   Printed in Hong Kong
First Edition   10 9 8 7 6 5 4 3 2 1

The whooping crane is one of America's largest and rarest birds.

Gallop, hop, climb, wiggle, swim — animals move in many different ways. A few kinds of animals get around by flying. Some insects such as butterflies and mosquitoes fly. Little mammals called bats fly. And birds fly. Big birds are special because they are the world's biggest flying animals.

A damselfly is an insect that travels by flying.

A large, fish-eating hawk called an osprey lands on its nest. Ospreys build onto the same nest of sticks year after year until it is very large.

2

Most big birds start life inside big eggs. Some species build big nests.

Some big birds have very long or very broad wings.

The director of education at the Tracy Aviary in Salt Lake City, Utah, holds a great horned owl. The wingspan of this species may be more than four and a half feet.

Some big birds have big feet on long legs. Some have long necks and some have long tails.

The long neck of a great blue heron.

The large feet and sharp talons of a snowy owl.

The big, forward-facing eyes of the great horned owl give it very sharp vision.

Some have big heads and big eyes.

Some have big bills.

DENISE CASEY

A white pelican has a very big bill.

Sandhill cranes in flight.

Big birds have adapted to live in many different habitats around the world, to eat many different kinds of food, to live alone or in flocks, to spend their lives flying or swimming or walking, to build enormous nests or hatch their eggs with no nest at all. The world's big birds are all unique creatures, but their big size makes them a special group.

Flying versus size

Flying is a wonderful way to travel. It gives birds the speed to escape from danger and the freedom to travel widely for seasonal foods, nesting, and warmth. Nearly every part of a flying bird's body is specially adapted to help it fly. Flying birds have compact, streamlined bodies; lightweight, hollow bones; very efficient breathing systems; strong hearts; and muscles that are devoted mainly to the activity of flying. Large flying birds have the most extreme specializations for flight.

Large size also has many advantages. Fewer animals attack big birds, and big birds can defend themselves and their eggs and chicks from bigger attackers than little birds can. Big birds can eat large, high-energy foods, such as whole fish and mice. It is also easier for big birds to maintain warm body temperatures because they have relatively more weight compared to the surface areas of their bodies than little birds.

A rough-legged hawk eats a mouse.

Gulls in flight.

But birds can't have both big size and the ability to fly at the same time. Flying requires a lot of energy, and thus birds that fly must be lightweight. But flying also requires strong muscles which can be quite heavy. About thirty-three pounds seems to be the size at which birds have the advantages of large size as well as the advantage of flight. The biggest flying birds all weigh about this amount, including swans and pelicans.

One of the largest flying animals in the world, the white pelican, weighs more than thirty pounds and spreads its wings more than nine feet from tip to tip.

A thin-walled, hollow bird bone. Notice the thin struts inside. They add strength while keeping the bone very lightweight.

Over aeons, birds have adapted to many different environments and ways of life. In this process, some bird species have lost the ability to fly, and at the same time, grown much bigger. Emperor penguins, for example, which are adapted to life in the sea and cannot fly, average

F.S. TODD/ VIREO

Emperor penguin with chick.

about sixty-five pounds, and the flightless elephant birds, now extinct, may have weigh-ed a thousand pounds!

This skeleton of the extinct giant moa is displayed in the Peabody Museum of Natural History at Yale University. Moas, which lived in New Zealand, and elephant birds, which lived in Mada-gascar, were both about ten feet tall, but moas weighed only half as much as elephant birds.

9

Big birds at sea

Many big birds live in or near the ocean. They depend on fish, squid, shrimp, and other sea creatures for food. Most of them build nests on beaches, cliffs, or trees on the seacoast or on islands.

Wandering albatrosses have the longest wings in the world — eleven and a half feet from tip to tip! Over the oceans of the Southern Hemisphere, they soar and glide above the waves and may remain aloft for hours, skillfully riding the wind currents. They are never seen on land except at their nesting places, usually on windy ocean islands. These white, web-footed birds catch squid and fish near the surface of the sea in their long, hooked bills. Wandering albatrosses may live as long as fifty years.

Wandering albatross.

11

Emperor penguins live in the southern oceans and only come onto the frozen pack ice near Antarctica to mate. After a female lays an egg, she returns to the sea to feed and leaves the egg with her mate. He keeps it warm for two months during the severe cold of the Antarctic winter by carrying it on top of his feet. His warm belly covers the top of the egg. These stately, four-foot-tall birds cannot fly. Their wings are shaped like flippers which enables them to swim after fish. On land or ice, they walk upright or scoot on their bellies.

W. J. L. SLADEN / VIREO

Emperor penguins scooting on their bellies.

A young brown pelican with a fish in its bill.

Brown pelicans have heavy bodies, long necks, and webbed feet. An enormous, elastic pouch is part of the lower jaw of their twelve-inch bills. They open their mouths underwater and scoop up two gallons of water and fish. When they return to the surface, they partly close their bills and spill the water out by tipping their bills straight down. Finally, they swallow the fish. Brown pelicans plunge-dive for fish along the American coasts of the Atlantic and Pacific oceans. They hold their wings back, crook their long necks, and splash loudly into the water. Air sacs in their breasts cushion them from the shock of hitting the water.

A cormorant dries its wings while nearby sea lions bask in the warm sunshine.

Highly social **cormorants** live in colonies along the seacoast in most parts of the world. They are big, blackish birds with long necks and thin, hooked beaks. They fly low over the water to find their prey. These expert swimmers then dive from the surface and chase fish to a depth of one hundred feet. In India, China, and Japan, cormorants have traditionally been trained on leashes to catch fish and carry them in their gullets to fishermen in boats. Cormorants often stand for long periods on land with their wings spread, drying them in the sun and wind.

Cormorants nest in large, densely packed colonies.

Colonies of gulls are often made up of different species. Here California gulls rest with darker Heermann's gulls along the Pacific Coast.

Screaming **gulls** circle by the thousands above seashores and harbors all over the world. Although some of the world's forty-plus species are only ten inches long, others grow up to thirty inches. Gulls are mostly white birds with streamlined bodies, long, narrow wings, and webbed feet. They are skilled fliers. These adaptable birds eat almost anything: they clean up beaches by eating dead fish, crabs, and worms; they follow fishing boats and eat the refuse thrown overboard; and they have sometimes saved farmers' crops by eating millions of grasshoppers. Gulls are very social. They roost and breed in enormous colonies, and they communicate with many calls and behaviors.

The pink-footed western gull lives along the Pacific Coast. It has a wingspan of four and a half feet. Gull chicks peck at the red spot of the adult's lower bill to beg for food.

17

Big birds of inland waters

Many big birds depend on the waters of ponds, rivers, marshes, or lakes instead of oceans. Most inland bodies of water have fresh water, while along the sea-coasts are vast areas of salty lagoons and wetlands. Some of the big birds that live on inland waters eat fish, shellfish, shrimp, or insects, and some eat plants that grow in the water and mud.

Trumpeter swans paddle gracefully near the shores of ponds. With a weight of thirty-three pounds, a length of five feet, and a wingspan of eight feet, they are among the largest flying birds in the world. They once ranged across North America, but these rare birds now remain only in Alaska, western Canada, and the northwestern United States. Some swans are also being moved to other parts of the continent where the species once lived. Swans mate for life: the male and female swim and eat together, build their nests in the reeds and grasses at the water's edge together, protect their eggs and raise their cygnets together.

Baby swans, called cygnets, weigh only a few ounces at hatching, but because they eat almost nonstop, they grow to twenty pounds within four months.

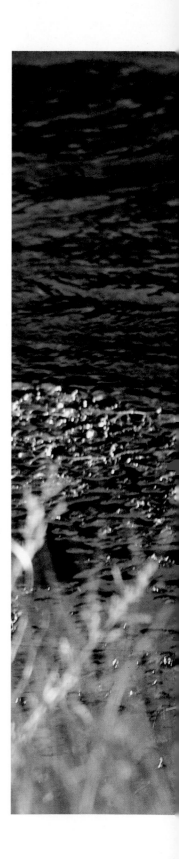

Great blue herons wade in the shallow water of ponds, marshes, and rivers across North America, in both fresh water and salt water. They nest in trees in colonies. Their nests are made of sticks. Wearing "bibs" of fine, long feathers over their breasts, these elegant blue-gray birds stalk their prey silently and slowly. Then, they swiftly grab fishes or frogs from the water with their pointed bills. In flight, their long necks are folded, their stiltlike legs trail behind them, and their wing beats are slow and stately.

An American bittern, a relative of the heron.

Great blue heron.

Bald eagle.

The symbol of the United States of America is a big bird — the **bald eagle**. It is a magnificent hunter with a white head and tail, sharp eyes, and a powerful yellow bill. Its wingspan is wider than a man can spread his arms. The bald eagle feeds mostly on fish from large rivers and lakes and along the seacoast. It builds a huge nest of sticks on a remote cliff or treetop and uses the same nest year after year. Although the bald eagle is endangered, its numbers are increasing.

The golden eagle, cousin of the bald eagle, hunts rabbits and mice on the grasslands, mountains, and deserts of North America, Europe, and Asia.

Tall, pink **flamingos** live on salty lagoons, shallow lakes, and mud flats in Africa, Asia, and South and Central America. Hundreds of thousands of these big birds may flock together, creating one of nature's most colorful spectacles. They wade in shallow water and swish their thick, down-curved bills through the water to filter out tiny creatures and plants to eat. During nesting, flamingo parents scoop up mud to build a nest up to eighteen inches high. The mud hardens to form a secure platform for their one egg, which is cared for by both parents.

The flamingo's bill is one of the most unusual in the bird world. The top jaw moves up and down, and the thick tongue helps pump water through ridges in the bill that strain out food.

These flamingos are pale pink, but some species are bright pink, red, or purplish.

The mating dance of sandhill cranes.

Sandhill cranes are tall, leggy, wading birds of the marshes and prairie wetlands of western North America. They eat grasshoppers, earthworms, crayfish, mice, eggs, grains, and other foods. In the spring, pairs of cranes dance their mating dance: they stretch their wings and bow to each other, they leap into the air, tossing their heads, and they strut grandly through the grass. Sandhill cranes migrate in flocks, and their constant calling in deep, hollow, rattling voices can often be heard before they can be seen high overhead.

Five-foot-tall sandhill cranes have white cheek patches and red "caps."

The V-formation helps Canada geese migrate. As each bird's body moves forward, it uplifts the air around it, and the uplifted air makes flying a little easier for the birds behind it. Thus, each bird can fly farther using less energy.

Big flocks of **Canada geese** migrate twice a year. In spring, they fly north to nest on lakes and marshes across Canada, Alaska, and the northernmost United States. In autumn, they return thousands of miles to their warm wintering grounds in the central and southern United States and northernmost Mexico. They mark the change of the seasons with their loud, hoarse honking and their V-formations crossing the skies. These heavy birds with their distinctive black heads and necks and white chin straps can often be seen feeding in fields of grain.

Parent leads goslings to the water when they are only one day old. They can already swim easily at this age.

Big birds on land

Many big birds live on land. They make nests on the ground, in trees, or on cliffs. Some are hunters that eat small animals, while others search for seeds, fruits, nuts, and other plant foods.

The biggest living bird in the world is the **ostrich**, reaching nine feet in height and weighing three hundred pounds. Ostriches can run forty miles per hour, faster than any other animals on two legs; a single stride may cover fifteen feet. They have powerful, muscular thighs and huge feet with only two toes. They cannot fly. Ostriches eat fruits, seeds, and leaves in their travels across the open plains and deserts of Africa. Their three-pound eggs are laid in shallow pits scratched in the ground and are tended by both parents until they hatch.

Ostrich.

An ostrich egg, the largest of any animal in the world, makes a chicken egg look small.

Male sage grouse.

Sage grouse are chunky birds that live in the foothills and plains of the American West. They are almost as big as turkeys. Sagebrush, a fragrant, gray-green shrub, is their main food. Every year, flocks of these big birds return to the same "strutling ground" to do their mating dances. Males puff up big orange air sacs on their breasts, fan the pointed feathers of their tails, and hold their wings away from their bodies. Looking very impressive, they strut among the other sage grouse and call out *bloop-bloop*. The females choose their mates and then lay their eggs in unlined nests scratched in the soil under sagebrush.

Many members of the grouse family, such as these white-tailed ptarmigan, use camouflage to hide. That means the color of the animal is the same as the background. Can you see the mother and two chicks? In winter, ptarmigan turn white to hide against the snow.

34

The **raven's** home is the wilderness of the American West, Alaska, and nearly all of Canada — from the frozen tundra to the seashore, in the mountains and forests, and across the deserts. The raven is the largest member of the songbird group, much larger than robins, warblers, or other well-known singing birds, but its "song" is a loud, hoarse croaking. Ravens are intelligent birds with good memories. If they cannot open the hard shells of shellfish or crabs, they fly up and drop them onto rocks to break the shells open. In captivity, they have even been taught to count.

Raven.

A great horned owl perches on a barn.

From its hidden perch among the treetops, the piercing yellow eyes and alert ears of a **great horned owl** can detect a mouse hundreds of yards away. Silently and swiftly, it dives on its prey. This fierce, solitary owl lives in a wide range of habitats across North America, and its prey includes insects, mice, rabbits, ducks, and

The barn owl is another big owl found across much of North America. Unlike the great horned owl, it has no upright feathers around its ears.

Two young owls have left the nest. They are still covered in downy feathers and are still fed by their parents.

pheasants. Although its wings spread four and a half feet from tip to tip, it weighs only three pounds. Yet, the great horned owl has been known to carry animals weighing nine pounds to its nestlings. The "horns" of this large owl are actually tufts of feathers.

A peacock's train — it's not really his tail — has dozens of colorful circles called "eye spots."

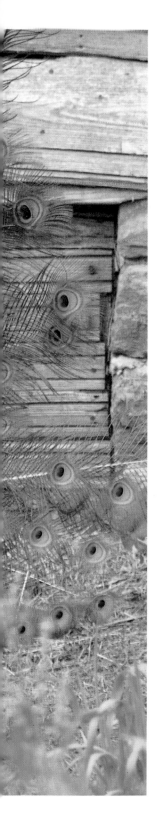

The brilliant, iridescent feathers of the **peacock** shimmer in the sunlight. His splendid, lacy train — fanned out to display to the peahen — is more than seven feet wide. In the wild, peafowl live in small groups in open forests in India, scratching seeds, berries, and insects from the forest floor. As evening approaches, they fly up into trees to roost, trumpeting loudly as they settle in for the night. Peafowl are easily domesticated, and they wander freely about many zoos and parks throughout the world.

The peacock's brilliant blue head has a little crown of stiff feathers.

39

The very rare **California condor** is one of the largest flying birds in the world, with broad wings spanning ten feet and a weight of twenty-five pounds. Its feathers are black, and the bare, bumpy skin on its head is bright orange. Condors soar in wide circles thousands of feet above the ground, lifted up by warm air currents. They eat the carcasses of dead animals and nest on canyon cliffs and mountain ledges of the West Coast. An intensive program to raise them in captivity and release them into their native habitat is helping prevent the extinction of this majestic species.

California condor at its nest.

Like its cousin the condor, the turkey vulture has no feathers on its head.

The common loon is a swimming and diving bird. Its call sounds like wild laughter.

There are many more species of big birds around the world
— colorful toucans with massive bills, native American turkeys, tall Australian emus with tiny wings, ocean-living gan-
nets, storks, loons, hawks, and many, many more. They are
not as easy to find as the many little birds that live in our
yards and gardens, in city parks, along fencerows in farm
country, or in forests, marshes, or other places. But seeing a
big bird is a special experience.

We may catch sight of geese flying overhead in migration or see flocks of gulls along the seacoast. Many zoos offer the chance to watch the behavior of some big bird species. There are also many wildlife refuges around the country where thousands of big birds of different species gather; here you can watch them in their native habitats.

The flight of the biggest birds is almost a miracle. Many adaptations balance their large size with their ability to fly. Big flightless birds also have unique adaptations to life on land or in the sea — no longer limited by the requirements of flight. Big birds are truly an amazing group.

Snow geese in flight.

42

Index